Once upon a time, on the hills of Shropshire and Welsh borders known as the Marches, there lived families of sheep.

They thrived, because, as they say "the land by here is lovely for sheep". The weather is ideal for growing lots of grass for them to eat. The fleece of the sheep makes high quality wool which has been in demand for hundreds of years.

This is the story of wool and wool trade and its importance to the making of Shrewsbury.

In times gone by everyone dressed in natural fabrics including linen from flax, leather, silk, cotton and wool from sheep.

Lambs are born in the spring and later the wool is collected from the older sheep using shears to give the sheep a wool cut.

Tangles are combed out and the wool is spun or twisted using a weight or spinning wheel to make long strands that can be rolled into balls.

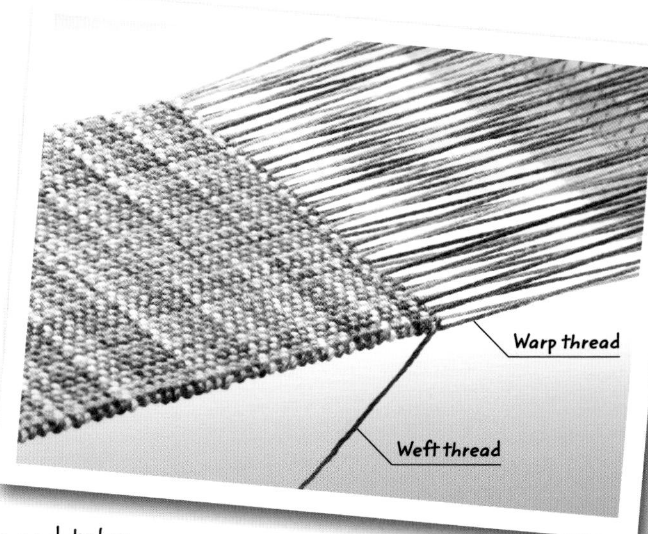

To make cloth the strands of wool are wound onto a loom, stretching the warp threads, the weft is threaded in and out of the warp at right angles, the result is cloth.

These methods have been used for hundreds of years and are still used today!

In times past the farmer weavers and their wives would weave lengths of cloth to about 40 metres long, about the length of three buses, and 0.75 metre wide, and then roll them up and take them to market.

An important trade grew up selling wool, fleeces and woven cloth.

5

In Shropshire, the border town of Oswestry was licensed as the staple, or market, to trade woollen cloth.

The traders from Shrewsbury, known as Drapers, would venture to the staple to buy the lengths of cloth from the farmers and local dealers.

The cloth that was traded in Oswestry came from all over North Wales and also from England. There were flannels, cottons and various grades of woollen cloth.

In those days before cheque books and credit cards were used, the Drapers had to carry large amounts of cash to buy the cloth.

The Drapers would set out from Shrewsbury, on horseback, early in the morning to meet at Nesscliffe.

They felt safer if they travelled together in groups as there was a risk of being robbed by highwaymen.

The most famous highwayman, Humphrey Kynaston, lived in a cave on the hills above Nesscliffe.

You can visit the site and see the steps leading up to the cave. Bats live in there today.

The Drapers brought the cloth back to Shrewsbury on packhorses to be processed, softened up and sometimes dyed into different colours.

Most of the work had to be done by hand and foot, as there were not many machines to help.

The "fullers" had the smelliest job; the cloth had to be put into barrels of urine collected from the people of Shrewsbury! The fullers would then jump on the wool for hours. This made the cloth, and the fullers feet, very soft. Afterwards the cloth was washed in the river.

Later, water powered fulling mills used hammers to soften the cloth.

After washing, the cloth was put out to dry on frames with hooks, called tenters, and was stretched tight, hence the expression to be on tenterhooks. Have you ever felt stretched and on tenterhooks?

The cloth would be worked with teasels, that were attached to a small paddle like a table tennis bat to raise a nap on the cloth. This made it softer to the touch and sell for a better price.

Have you seen teasels growing in the wild?

The Shearmen then came along and tidied up the newly stretched and softened cloth and trimmed all the loose ends off.

When the cloth was finished, it was taken to the Market Hall, in the Square in Shrewsbury.

In 1596 this was the New Market Hall. The Drapers traded the cloth on the first floor, on the ground floor there was a corn market and fruit and vegetable were sold in the open in the square.

The crest of Queen Elizabeth I was put on the New Market Hall.

Can you find the crest and see a red dragon and check the date?

When the woollen cloth had been sold it was loaded on to pack horses and taken to London, it took four days to get there. The cloth was sold again to the London Drapers and it was exported to Europe and America. There was an important market in Rouen across the sea in France.

Later, when Bristol became a place where the cloth could be sold, it was shipped in boats called Severn Trows.

These boats had flat bottom so they could still be used when the water in the River Severn was low. Men, bow hauliers, who used long ropes and pulleys to pull the boats up and down stream had to drag the trows over mud sometimes.

The cloth was taken down stream and then on the return journey the trows brought back teasels from Somerset and wine and spirits from Europe.

Many of the boats were based in Frankwell near the old Welsh Bridge.

In this area of the town many people associated with the wool trade worked. The fullers and dyers needed water to wash the cloth whilst they worked with it, so the logical place to use was the River Severn. Dyers used plants and fruits to make natural dyes to colour the cloth.

Everybody had their own job to do and they got together in trade Guilds or Companies. They kept the skills to themselves and would only share that knowledge with other people who did the same job. They trained young people called apprentices.

Other trades including Fellmongers and Shearmen had their own trade guilds and meeting places. Fellmongers Hall is a building that has survived but the guild does not function in Shrewsbury today.

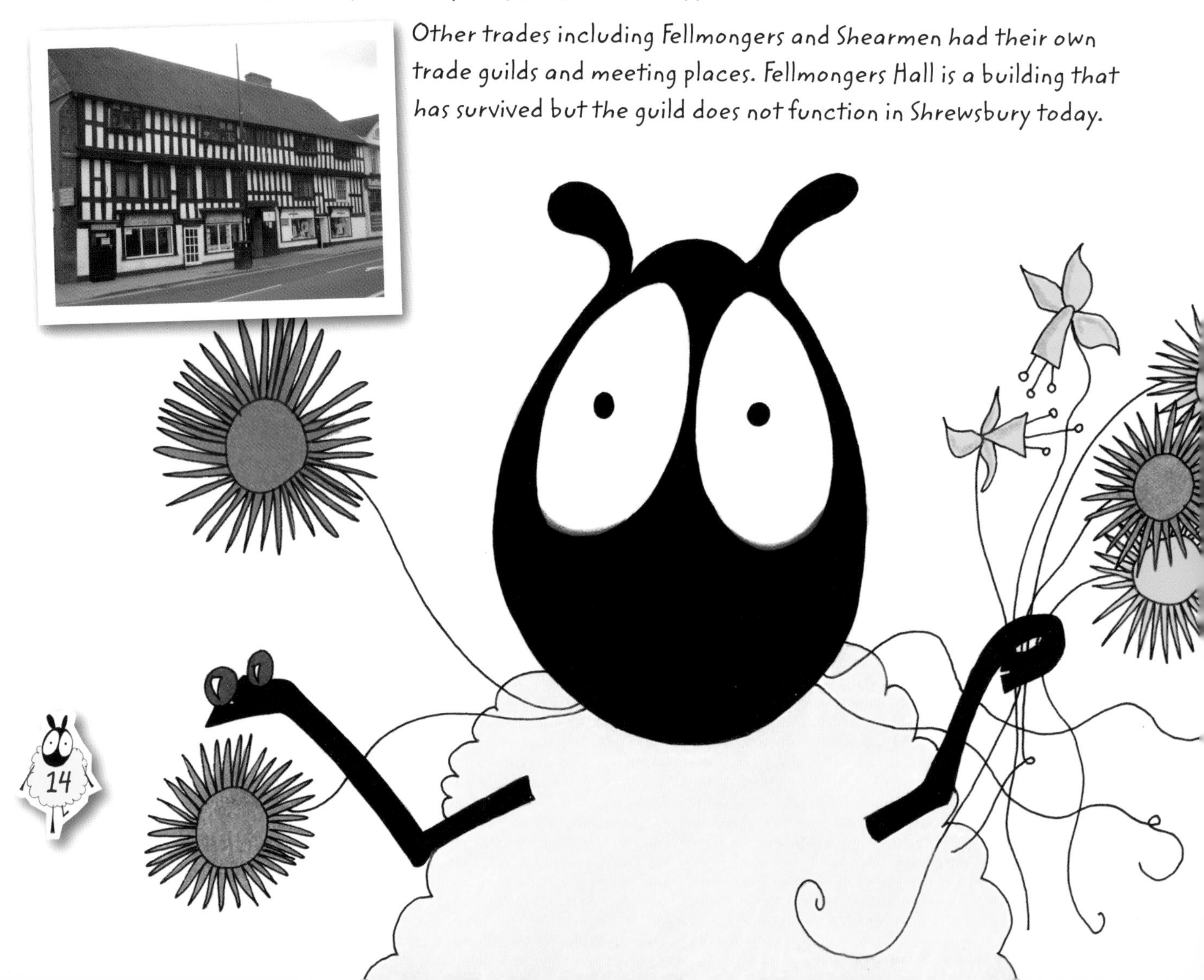

The Shearmen`s Hall was in Milk St, there is no trace of the old building above ground level other than the name on the building and it is currently used as a coffee bar. The Shearman had their chapel in St Julian`s Church nearby in the High St.

Although the Drapers relied on the Shearmen to finish the cloth before sale, there was great rivalry between the guilds and the Drapers refused to let the Shearmen share the trade in cloth and prevented them and any other interlopers from other guilds from sharing in the profitable trade.

Shropshire damsons are good for dying things red.

Because the Drapers controlled the trade many of them became wealthy and built large town houses which have remained in use for over 400 years.

Here are two views of William Rowley`s house, the early timber frame building may have been used as a warehouse and the other is one of the first brick built houses in Shrewsbury in 1618.

Rowley`s House is being used as a museum until the new museum is ready have you visited it yet?

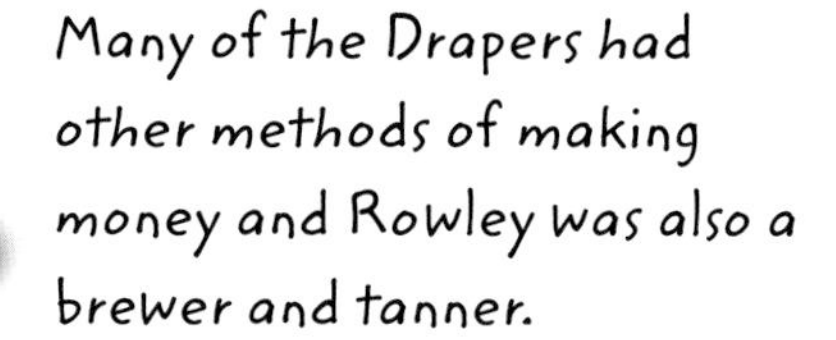

Many of the Drapers had other methods of making money and Rowley was also a brewer and tanner.

Richard Owen was another Draper and he had a mansion built in the Square.

Can you see the stone with his name on it and a date? What are the spikes for?

The great wealth accumulated meant that some Drapers became involved with charitable work and in 1444 they established some social housing in front of the the north side of St Mary`s Church in what was known as Ox Lane.

These so called Alms Houses were for widows and spinsters who received money, fuel and clothing from Drapers.

They lived in timber framed cottages with a common hall. Degory Watur lived in the warden`s house in the early days and financial support came from Katherine Bonel the widow of a former Draper.

Here is a picture of Edward IV who granted the founding Charter to the Shrewsbury Drapers Company in January 1462.

As well as Charitable works the Drapers enjoyed good food and wine and in 1575 they rebuilt Drapers Hall to have meetings and entertainment.

This fine table was built inside the Hall in about 1635 and cost £2.17.6d. which is £2 87, it would cost a lot more today.

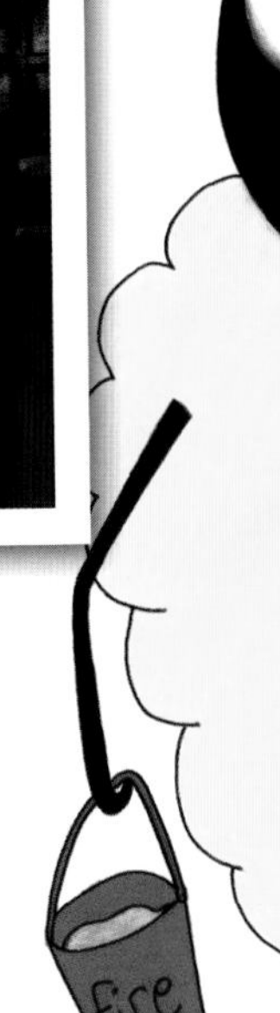

The Shrewsbury Drapers Company today 550 years on

The links with the origins of the Company continue today with the ownership of the Hall and the continuing support of local charities.

The Hall is one of the few original guild halls still in use for its original purpose and much of the furniture including the tables and benches are also in daily use it is also one of the few Guild Halls you can visit as it now used as a popular restaurant.

Today there are 80 members who are actively involved with the charitable work of the Company which includes raising funds for the maintenance of the alms houses and supporting an annual textile design competition and other charities nominated by the Master of the year.

There are now 25 people living in three groups of almshouses in Shrewsbury and this link of providing homes for people has also continued for over 550 years.

Since 1995 the Company has run a Textile Design Competition for people and students living in Shropshire and following judging there is an annual exhibition of the entries in September in the Drapers Chapel in St Mary`s Church in the Shrewsbury.

The company continues to thrive.

The legacy of the wool trade can be seen all over many English market Towns in the names of the streets and public houses and in Shrewsbury the legacy is seen in many of the fine timber frame and stone buildings that remain.